P9-CAD-721

BOYS DANCING

From School Gym to Theater Stage

George Ancona

CANDLEWICK PRESS

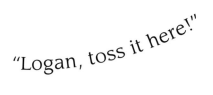

"Swing, Raptor, swing!"

"Ely, get the ball!"

"Logan, toss it here!"

"Hey Ryan, run!"

It's spring, and the weather is warm enough for students to go out on the playground for recess. The boys have twenty minutes to run, jump, yell, climb, and throw balls to one another. They never stop moving.

Starting at the beginning of the school year, Pamela, a dance teacher, and Brian, a piano player, visit several schools in town once a week. They come from the National Dance Institute of New Mexico (NDI New Mexico). The students attend classes that take place in their schools' gyms. They learn to leap, run, spin, jump, and show emotions like joy or anger . . . all to music.

The lessons teach the students to dance and prepare them for performances that will take place in May. This year's show is called *Imagine the Possibilities.* It will have twenty-two acts that celebrate famous books through song and dance. Preparing for the number called "Treasure Island," Pamela shows the students how to look like angry pirates.

By April, teams of students from different schools come together to rehearse. They are organized by grades. Raptor, Logan, Ely, and Ryan are dancing together.

When the students become too noisy to hear Pamela, she claps her hands— *1, 2 . . . 1, 2, 3.* Then the students clap back the same rhythm—*1, 2 . . .1, 2, 3*— and they quiet down.

Sometimes the gyms get so crowded with dancers that students have to practice in the halls.

Students who are especially enthusiastic in their dancing are chosen to be part of a team that meets on Saturdays at The Dance Barns. These students get extra training. Ely, Raptor, Logan, and Ryan are part of a team called Boys Ballet Boot Camp. The first thing they do is to put on their soft-soled dance shoes.

Then they warm up by running through the halls of The Dance Barns. Mark, one of the teachers, has the boys do pull-ups to strengthen their arms.

Mark and Allegra teach the boys ballet. The classes begin with stretches on the floor and exercises at the barre. The boys build up strength as they turn, leap, and do ballet steps.

Logan learns how to dance with Allegra as his partner. This is called a *pas de deux.* Mark shows the boys how to leap by having them jump over him.

Diana teaches a tap-dance class for older students. Metal taps on the soles of their shoes ring out with each step, like musical instruments. Tap is music and dance all in one.

Each dance number has its own music and choreography. Emily is choreographing the opening dance. She moves pieces of paper around on the floor to show the dancers where they should be and where they should go. They use books and a book cart as props to help create the movements of the dancer.

There is a pirate fight in "Treasure Island." Ambrose was invited to train the boys on how to fake fistfights. The class begins with Ambrose pretending to punch Emily. Then she punches him back. They never touch each other, but it looks like they do. The boys have so much fun that they end each fight laughing. Nobody gets hurt.

The older boys were also trained by Ambrose to fight with swords. Bert plays the music for the fight.

The boys have to be strong to flip the girls safely.

Liz trains the boys to make mean and angry faces for the "Treasure Island" fights. The dance studio mirrors are ideal for Logan, Riley, and Ely to show faces that make everybody laugh.

Pamela rehearses the class with Logan, Ryan, and Raptor for the happy and playful dance based on *The Adventures of Tom Sawyer* by Mark Twain.

With the performance just weeks away, all the teams are rehearsing together with their teachers while Kevin plays the piano.

Ely gets to dance with a partner.
Ryan and Raptor sing with the teams,
and they all practice their scary faces.

Jindra directs some of the older boys in a rehearsal of "Treasure Island." Bert plays the music for the dance. Meanwhile, the cast gets bigger and bigger as more school teams join the rehearsals.

About a week before the performance, there is a dress rehearsal. Ryan, Raptor, and Logan try on the overalls they will wear for "The Adventures of Tom Sawyer." The students practice changing their costumes between each dance.

Bert conducts the orchestra and singers for the dress rehearsal.
Parts of the score are from films, musicals, and popular songs.
Other parts were composed just for this performance.

The dancers, the orchestra, the stage crew, and the lighting technicians work together to put on the show. The next time they all perform will be in front of an audience.

The day of the performance arrives. The two studios are transformed into one large theater. Half of the space is the stage; the other half is the audience. The performance begins with runs and jumps and the opening dance with the whole cast.

Next, the book *Oh, the Places You'll Go!*
by Dr. Seuss is read. This sets the stage for
the next twenty dances to be performed,
all of them based on books.

Each year, one kindergarten class participates in the performance. Here they perform "Wild Things," based on Maurice Sendak's *Where the Wild Things Are.*

The older boys, including Raptor, perform "Treasure Island," based on the classic story by Robert Louis Stevenson. This action-packed dance features fight routines they learned.

Girls fill the stage in colorful costumes for a dance based on *The Thousand and One Nights,* a collection of stories that includes the tales of Ali Baba and the forty thieves, Scheherazade, and Sinbad the Sailor.

Boys wearing turbans follow the girls across the stage
to finish this vibrant dance.

"The Adventures of Tom Sawyer" opens with Logan sitting and reading a book by a fence.

Soon Logan is joined by boys and girls dressed in costumes that reflect life along the Mississippi River in 1876. Logan, Ely, Raptor, and Ryan are all onstage for this jolly dance.

"New Mexico Folktales" celebrates the culture, people, food, music, and dance of New Mexico. The theater looks and sounds like a lively fiesta.

Then Sherlock Holmes is celebrated. The stage is covered with little detectives who try to solve the mysteries that surround them.

The detectives are guided and in some cases carried by members of the local fire department. Parents, teachers, and firefighters from the community participate in this annual event.

After more than twenty dances are performed, the grand finale features all five hundred students, including Logan, Ely, Ryan, and Raptor, with teachers, parents, and firefighters, all dancing and singing onstage. It was a lot of hard work, but also a lot of good times and fun.

To Emily Lowman

THANKS
To Roy McKeag, who was never too busy to cross the arroyo to help, and Peter Ellzey,
a friend and master tech.

THE TEACHERS
Melissa Briggs-Bransford, Tara Debevec, Ambrose Ferber, Pamela Ladas, Allegra Lillard,
Emily Lowman, Jindra McIntosh, Mark Morgan, Diana Orozco-Garrett, Liz Salganek

THE SCHOOL MUSICIANS
Brian Bennett, Bert Dalton, Kevin Ward

THE SCHOOLS
Acequia Madre Elementary School, Carlos Gilbert Elementary School, Gonzales Community School,
Tesuque Elementary School

THE PARENTS, FAMILIES & COMMUNITY MEMBERS . . .
who drop off, pick up, and cheer on their kids. And the firefighters who participated in the performance.

THE BEGINNING
Jacques d'Amboise, a dancer with the New York
City Ballet, founded the National Dance Institute
in 1976. He created the program especially to
engage neighborhood boys in the arts. NDI New
Mexico was cofounded by Catherine Oppenheimer
in 1994. NDI New Mexico believes that through
dance children are able to develop discipline,
a standard of excellence, and a belief in them-
selves that can carry over into their future life.

Text and photographs copyright © 2017 by George Ancona. All rights reserved. No part of this book may be reproduced, transmitted, or stored in an information retrieval system in any form
or by any means, graphic, electronic, or mechanical, including photocopying, taping, and recording, without prior written permission from the publisher. First edition 2017. Library of Congress
Catalog Card Number 2015909413. ISBN 978-0-7636-8202-6. This book was typeset in Leawood.
Candlewick Press, 99 Dover Street, Somerville, Massachusetts 02144. visit us at www.candlewick.com.
Printed in Shenzhen, Guangdong, China. 17 18 19 20 21 22 CCP 10 9 8 7 6 5 4 3 2 1